ANALYSIS OF THE LEGISLATIVE RESPONSES TO CYBER PORNOGRAPHY AGAINST CHILDREN

VOLUME 2, ISSUE 1 OF BRILLOPEDIA

BHAVANA SHARMA

Contents

Preface

"Start writing, no matter what. The water does not flow until the faucet is turned on".

• Louis L'Amour

Hundreds of students and professors are contributing their work to Brillopedia, we are here to provide ample information about Law and Contemporary issues. Our aim is to provide a platform for today's generation to express their views and ideas on law and contemporary law.

CHAPTER ONE

ABSTRACT

Over the past two decades, information and communication technologies have advanced at an accelerating rate. Information andcommunication technologies have recently made tremendous advancements that have benefited both kids and adults in terms of socialising, education, and enjoyment. Specifically, the growth of Information and communication technologies has offered Using the Internet and related technologies to create new venues for interaction and collaboration with kids and teenagers, Peer-to-peerwebsites, social networking sites, and chat rooms are examples of places where people may interact socially. These technical advancements have concurrently made it possible for violence, especially violence against children, to be committed by, with, and through the use of Information and communication technologies.[1] As a result, children who use the Internet and related technologies are more likely to be the victims of child abuse and exploitation made possible by Information and Communication Technologies, which is frequently difficult to identify and stop. This study provides an overview of the country's legislative responses to the online child. Abuse and exploitation, with a particular focus on activities related to child pornography (also known as "child", abuse images"), online grooming and cyberbullying.[2] This study focused on the following: 1) Analysis Legislative measures to address violence against children committed with and through Information and Communication Technologies' alignment with relevant equipment; 2) To set examples of good practice in a legal competence National level environment for child online safety in compliance with relevant standards; and 3) to highlight the recommendations for strengthening the legal framework to handle Information and Communication Technologies facilitation.An analysis of child abuse and exploitation in the country was done.

Keywords: Information Technology, Cybercrime, Children, Internet, Cyber-Pornography.

[1]Cybercrime: protecting children from online abuse and exploitation, United Nations: Office on Drugs and Crime, //www.unodc.org/unodc/en/frontpage/2015/July/cybercrime_-protecting-children-from-online-abuse-and-exploitation.html (last visited Sep 26, 2022).

[2]ibid

CHAPTER TWO

INRODUCTION

Over the past 20 years, information and communication technologies have advanced quickly. Both adults and children may now take use of previously unheard-of chances and advantages in terms of socialising, education, and enjoyment thanks to recent rapid advancements in information and communication technologies. Particularly, the growth of information and communication technologies has given kids and teenagers who use the Internet and related technologies1 new places to socialise and establish connections, such chat rooms, peer-to-peer websites, and social networking sites. In the meanwhile, technical advancement has made it possible for crimes to be perpetrated via information and communication technologies, especially crimes against minors. Children and teenagers who use the Internet and related technologies are more susceptible than adults to online abuse and exploitation. First off, kids and teenagers who use the Internet and related technologies are sometimes ill-prepared to properly comprehend the possibility of being exposed to unlawful acts carried out via the use of information and communication technologies. It may also be challenging for parents, guardians, and caregivers to keep tabs on their children's online activities due to the rapid advancement of technology and the fact that kids typically absorb new technologies more quickly than adults.

Law enforcement organisations find it more difficult to spot suspicious activity, identify offenders, investigate, and prosecute illegal activities against children when such activities are committed by the use of Information and Communication Technologies. This is because technological advancements allow Internet users to surf anonymously on websites powered by the Tor network and engage in electronic transactions by using virtual currencies, which are not easily governed by existing laws and regulations. To combat the multifaceted danger that cybercrime poses,

a comprehensive strategy must be used, including the adoption of laws and
regulations, awareness-raising, capacity-building, and technical help.

CHAPTER THREE

OBJECTIVE AND METHODOLOGY

Objective

This study supports legislative actions in an effort to improve child protection. to fight the country's use of Information and communication technologies to assist child exploitation and abuse. Therefore, it seeks to: 1) Provide analysis of domestic law in alignment with pertinent instruments; 2) Provide examples of current good legal practises for child online protection at the national level that are compliant with the pertinent international standard; and 3) Strengthen the nation's legal framework to address issues of online child abuse and exploitation.

Methodology

This Research Paper bashed on Doctrinalapproach research which primary and secondarydata on Regional Study examines legislative responses that address Information and communication technologies facilitated child abuse and exploitation with a primary focus on: 1) activities related to child pornography (also known as "child abuse images"), the most common forms of violence against children committed by, with, and through the use of Information and communication technologies.

The primary law that addresses acts related to child pornography in electronic form is the Information Technology Act (enacted in 2000 and amended by the Information Technology (Amendment) Act, 2008) (hereafter also referred to as "IT Act"). The Protection of Children from Sexual Offenses Act (enacted in 2012) also contains provisions criminalizing: a) using a child for pornographic purposes; and b) storing any pornographic material in any form involving a child for commercial purposes. Furthermore, the Penal Code (enacted in 1860 and last amended by the Criminal Law (Amendment) Act, 2013) has several provisions addressing various obscenity offenses, which may also be applicable to offenses involving child pornography.Many pornography websites are banned in India. But websites that are registered in other countries are outside the purview of Indian law. But you cannot keep such content by saving, it also comes under the category of crime. Cyber pornography plays a minor role in problematic social issues such as child abuse, violence against women, assault, inequality, family and relationship problems, youth mistreatment, incest and physically contagious diseases. Dirty content distributed on cyberspace has made India's old laws problematic. There is no control over what appears on the web with the click of a mouse button due to the absence of jurisdictional boundaries and the sheer amount of traffic that the Internet can handle.

CHAPTER FOUR

CHILD PORNOGRAPHY

According to the Protection of Children from Sexual Offenses Act, "child pornography in any form" is defined as "any form of media" that "uses a child" for sexual gratification. This includes: (a) any depiction of a child's sexual organs; (b) any depiction of a child engaging in real or simulated sexual acts (with or without penetration); and (c) any indecent or obscene representation of a child. According to Section 15 of the POCSO Act, which criminalises the storage of such material for profit, "child pornography in any form" is also known as "pornographic material in any form involving a child." The word "any type of media" used in Section 13 of the Protection of Children from Sexual Offenses Act encompasses broadcast television programmes and Internet ads as well as printed and electronic media.

The phrase "use a kid" refers to using a child in any way, including print, electronic, computer, or any other technology, to prepare, produce, provide, transmit, publish, facilitate, or distribute pornographic content, according to the Explanation to Section 13 of this Act. According to Section 67B of the IT Act, "child pornography in electronic form" refers to any content that: (a) shows children engaging in sexually explicit behaviour; or (b) shows children in an obscene, indecent, or sexually explicit way. The IT Act's Section 67B makes certain actions involving such materials illegal.

The Explanation to Section 13 of this Act further articulates that the expression "use a child" means involving a child through any medium like print, electronic, computer, or any other technology for preparation, production, offering, transmitting, publishing, facilitation, and distribution of the pornographic material. Pursuant to Section 67B of the IT Act, "child pornography in electronic form" includes any material in any electronic form that: (a) depicts children engaged in a sexually explicit act or conduct; or (b) depicts children in an obscene or indecent or sexually explicit manner. Section 67B of the IT Act criminalizes prescribed activities related to such materials. With respect to defining the term "obscenity" referred to in Section 67B of the IT Act, Section 67 of the IT Act provides which materials may be deemed "obscene" as stated below. Material in any electronic form may be considered obscene if it is lascivious or appeals to the prurient interest or if its effect is, or (where it comprises two or more distinct items) the effect of any one of its items, is, if taken as a whole, such as to tend to deprave and corrupt persons who are likely, having regard to all relevant circumstances, to read, see, or hear the matter contained or embodied in it.

CHAPTER FIVE

AGE OF POTENTIAL VICTIM OF ACTIVITIES RELATED TO CHILD PORNOGRAPHY

Indian law considers everyone under 18 years of age as a potential victim of child pornography offenses, regardless of the age of sexual consent. With regard to child pornography in electronic form, the Explanation to Section 67B of the IT Act states that for the purpose of this section, "children" refers to persons who have not completed the age of 18 years. With respect to child pornography in any form, Section 2 (1) (d) of the Protection of Children from Sexual Offenses Act states that in this Act, unless the context otherwise requires, "child" means any person below the age of 18 years. In India, the age of consent to sexual intercourse is 18 years for women pursuant to Section 375 of the Penal Code (amended by the Criminal Law (Amendment) Act, 2013).

Country that possibly embraces virtual images and sexually exploitative representations of children related to child pornography offenses under its domestic law Section 67B (b) of the IT Act specifically punishes anyone who creates text or digital "images" or collects, browses, downloads, seeks, advertises, promotes, exchanges, or distributes material in any electronic form depicting children in an obscene or indecent or sexually explicit manner. In addition, Section 67B of the IT Act applies to sexually exploitative representations of children including any book, pamphlet, paper, writing, drawing, painting, "representation" or figure in electronic form.Accessing and viewing of child pornography have explicit provisions that criminalize accessing or viewing child pornography under their domestic legislation; and Section 67B (b) of the IT Act explicitly criminalizes browsing any material in any electronic form, which depicts children in an obscene or indecent or sexually explicit manner.

Country that possibly criminalizes acts constituting online grooming India Although Indian law does not use the explicit term "online grooming", Section 12 of the Protection of Children from Sexual Offenses Act punishes any person who commits sexual harassment upon a child by repeatedly or constantly following or watching or contacting a child either directly or through electronic, digital, or any other means with sexual intent as mentioned in Section 11 of this Act. Moreover, Section 67B (c) of the IT Act makes it an offense to induce, cultivate, or entice children into an online relationship with one or more children for sexually explicit acts. In addition, Section 67B (d) of the IT Act criminalizes facilitating online child abuse.

However, the term "facilitate abusing children online" is neither specified nor explained in the IT Act. The general wording "facilitates abusing children online" under Section 67B (d) of the IT Act may cover online grooming unless there is an impediment to the punishment of a preparatory act and with some concerns in respect of overcriminalization.84 Indian law considers everyone under age 18 as a potential victim of online grooming and related activities. Section 2 (1) (d) of the Protection of Children from Sexual Offenses Act states that "child" means any person below the age of 18 years. In addition, the Explanation to Section 67B of the IT Act states that for the purposes of this Section, the term "children" refers to persons who have not yet completed 18 years of age.

CHAPTER SIX

INDIA HAS DATA RETENTION PROVISIONS WITH A SPECIFIED: A SPECIFIED DATA RETENTION PERIOD

Section 79 (2) (c) of the IT Act provides that intermediaries are exempted from liability for third party content provided that they observe due diligence while discharging their duties under this Act and also observe such other guidelines as the Central Government may prescribe. The Information Technology (Guidelines for Cyber Cafe) Rules were issued in exercise of powers conferred by Section 79 (2) of the IT Act in order to establish the Government's standard for what constitutes "due diligence" by intermediaries. These Rules contain provisions addressing the duties of cybercafé owners, as one of the intermediaries, to retain prescribed information as part of their duty to observe due diligence under Section 79 (2) of the IT Act as stated below. In addition, cybercafé owners shall be responsible for storing and maintaining: a) a history of websites accessed using the computer resources at the cybercafe; and b) logs of proxy servers installed at the cybercafé for each user or for each access for a period of at least one year pursuant to Section 5 of the Information Technology (Guidelines for Cyber Cafe) Rules.

CHAPTER SEVEN

REQUIREMENT TO IDENTIFY USERS OF PUBLIC COMPUTERS IN CYBERCAFES

Cybercafes shall not allow any user to use its computer resource without the identity of the user being established pursuant to Section 4(1) of the Information Technology (Guidelines for Cyber Cafe) Rules. The intending user may establish his identify by producing a document which shall identify the user to the satisfaction of the cybercafe. Such document may include any of the following: 1) identity card issued by any school or college; 2) photo credit card or debit card issued by a bank or post office; 3) passport; 4) voter identity card; 5) permanent account number (PAN) card issued by income-tax authority; 6) photo identity card issued by the employer or any government agency; 7) driver's license issued by the appropriate government; or 8) unique identification (UID) number issued by the unique identification authority of India (UIDAI). A cybercafe must keep a record of the user identification document by storing either a photocopy or a scanned copy of the document duly authenticated by the user and an authorized representative of the cybercafe. Such record shall be securely maintained for a period of at least one year according to Section 4 (2) of the Information Technology (Guidelines for Cyber Cafe) Rules.

CHAPTER EIGHT

LEGISLATION THAT SPECIFICALLY ADDRESSES THE USE OF INFORMATION AND COMMUNICATION TECHNOLOGIES TO COMMIT CRIMES AGAINST CHILDREN

The principal law that governs crimes against children committed by the use of ICTs in India is the Information Technology Act (amended by the Information Technology (Amendment) Act, 2008) (also known as "IT Act"). Section 67B (b) of the IT Act criminalizes downloading or browsing of material in electronic form depicting children in an obscene or indecent or sexually explicit manner.

CRIMINAL LIABILITY OF CHILDREN INVOLVED IN PORNOGRAPHY

Moreover, criminal liability must focus on an adult offender, who is responsible for the exploitation of a child and on the crimes he/she committed against that child. Accordingly, it is important to analyses the minimum age for criminal responsibility under domestic law as country may punish child offenders involved in pornography because they are criminally liable.Indian Penal Code only deals with child pornography offenses – govern crimes involving pornography or obscenity under their domestic law (whether Criminal Codes/Penal Codes or special laws) as stated above Analysis of the legislative responses to crimes against children in alignment with relevant international instruments. Legislation regarding child pornography, Legislation specific to child pornography. India do not address the criminal liability of children involved in pornography in cases of child victims, not child offenders.

However, there has also been a concerning surge in cybercrime in India along with the increased internet access. What is more alarming is the epidemic-like spread of a particular type of cybercrime: spreading pornographic material starring women without their permission. The problem was recently brought to light when screenshots from an Instagram group called Bois Locker Room—the term bois is a variant of the word lads—created by adolescent males were leaked during a national lockdown. there was Based on the screenshots, it appeared that these adolescent boys were sharing morphed pictures of minor girls, objectifying them and passing derogatory remarks.

In India's societal structure, sex is a contentious topic that is frequently associated with obscene and immoral behaviour. The present legal framework forbids the sale, appropriation, and public display of offensive or explicit content. Protection of public profound quality and credibility is the primary priority here. The right to watch, examine, or admire pornography (which might be added to his ability to talk freely and articulately or perhaps the privilege to protection under the Indian constitution) is restricted by such regulations, which impinge on an individual's individual freedom and good autonomy. This article aims to determine if there are any clear standards of vulgarity that may be used to evaluate a right to pornography.

While pornography is available in print periodicals in India, it is primarily consumed online. This usage is growing as cell phones and the internet are becoming more widely used. Despite the increased admission, public discussion and viewpoints on pornography remain muted and taboo in many parts of India. Distributing or transmitting explicit content is prohibited in India.[1] In India, web pornography has become immensely popular, accounting for anything between 30% and 70% of all traffic. For telecom companies, it has grown to be a substantial source of traffic and information revenue. A well-known pornographic website provided information on viewing, and the public capital Delhi saw up to 40% of all visitors. According to a self-reporting study, 63% of teenagers in urban areas, like Haryana, admitted to seeing pornography, with 74% of them accessing it via their mobile devices. More people in India will genuinely want to surreptitiously see pornography as mobile phone and internet access continue to grow. Half of Indian Internet traffic has been discovered by Quartz to often access popular pornographic websites on mobile devices. As the internet becomes more readily available to the average inhabitant, online sensual comedies have also become popular in India.

[1]Susanna Paasonen, Carnal Resonance: Affect and Online Pornography (Cambridge, Mass; London: MIT Press, 2011).

REVENGE PORN

Revenge porn refers to the publication of any person's private life activities, such as sexual material, either photos or videos, without their consent for the purpose of making them public so as to cause embarrassment to them. Images are sometimes accompanied by personal information about the subject, including the person's full name, address, and links to their social media profiles. Now to take revenge on a person in India, he is being maligned in ways like revenge pornography by wrongly using his name and photo. Most of the children under the age of 18 are involved in this. Often children get caught in someone's false love and share many such memories of their personal life with each other. Children have tried to show their love by sharing many photos and videos. But they forget that the data shared by them will not be misused and in the end most of the children are the victims of this.

Case study:1Revenge porn Case Valsad (Gujrat)

In one of the recent case in April 2015, a 21-year-old man was booked by the police in the Nargol village of Valsad (Gujarat) for allegedly spreading photographs of his teenage ex-girlfriend in compromising positions on popular social media sites. The pictures were reportedly taken on a mobile phone but were posted by the accused when the girl's parents were reportedly looking for a groom for the girl. The accused was charged with molestation under different sections of the Information Technology Act and the Protection of Children from Sexual Offences Act.While revenge porn essentially creates sexual violence against girls and women, it necessarily involves voyeurism, hacking, stalking, and violation of privacy. There is no specific law for revenge porn but the offences can be regulated by applying Section 354C, IPC (Voyeurism), Section 66E, IT Act (violation of privacy) and Section 509, IPC (harming the modesty of women). Revenge porn should also be seen in the perspective of indecent representation of women.

Case Study: 2 MMS case Related of an Adivasi Girl in Birbhum[1]

A 16-year-old tribal girl, who worked as a daily wage labourer to support her parents in Birbhum (West Bengal), was punished by the local panchayat for falling in love with a non-tribal boy from a nearby village in June 2010. She was stripped publicly, made to walk around the village for about two hours, sexually harassed by random villagers and photographed and videoed. These photographs and videos were sent as multi-media messages (MMS) to everyone in the village to ensure that no other village girl would dare to repeat her crime. No one including the authorities at the nearby Mohammad BazzarPolicstation, came to her rescue and her shocked parents were of little assistance. She made her way back home only to be taunted by her neighbours and others. No case was registered against her attackers and no one defied the tribal panchayat'sdiktat. The evidence was tampered with, as community leaders were involved in the crime. The girl spent a couple of months neglected and in isolation and then mustered the courage to lodge a complaint against those who had sexually harassed, violated and ostracized her. In doing so, she stood alone against the advice of her parents, family and friends. She reported the incident to the police and lodged a formal complaint, but there was no evidence except for the MMS. No one was willing to testify. Two days after filing the complaint, the six main accused were arrested. Fearing a backlash from the community, the victim was sent to a government welfare home in Rampurhat. She continues to live there. Although she was honoured by the President of India with the National Bravery Award for standing up against the panchayat-like body, she leads a life of isolation and ostracism. She has not been able to go home as many members of her family refuse to speak to her. Nonetheless, the district administration has arranged for her education, while women's organizations are demanding her rehabilitation in the community. The girl wants to finish her studies and fight for the rights of others who have been similarly abandoned

[1]The Hindu News Paper

CHAPTER TEN

LEGISLATIVE PROVISION COMBATING CHILD PORNOGRAPHY IN INDIA

1. Under Protection of Children from Sexual Offences Act, 2012 (POCSO)[1]

The POCSO Act criminalises the use of children for pornographic purposes. Now, section 13 of the Act explains what actions are considered to be the usage of a kid for pornographic purposes. The aforementioned provision states that anybody who exploits a kid for sexual enjoyment through any written or electronic medium, whether it was intended for public consumption or merely for personal use, is considered to have exploited the child for pornographic activities. This includes showing a kid's sexual organs, portraying a child in an offensive way, and involving a youngster in actual or simulated sexual behaviour without first forcing them to be Penetrated.

Anyone violating Section 13 of the POCSO Act is subject to a minimum 5-year jail sentence as well as a fine under Section 14. Additionally, if the same offence is found to have been committed again, the offender faces a minimum sentence of 7 years in jail as well as a fine. In addition, it states that if a person engages in pornographic activity while also breaking the law under sections 3 or 5 or 7 or 9, they will also be breaking section 14 of the POCSO Act and will be penalised under sections 4 or 6 or 8 or 10 of the law, accordingly.

Additionally, the POCSO Act's Section 15 imposes penalties for keeping or having pornographic material that depicts a kid in any of three possible scenarios. First off, sharing such material with the intent to conduct child pornography is penalised by a minimum punishment of Rs. 5000, and if the crime is repeated, it is penalised by a minimum fine of Rs. 10,000. Second, if the storage or possession was done in order to show or distribute it, then the offender faces up to three years in jail, a fine, or both.

However, if the storage was done with the intention of reporting or utilising it as evidence in court, it would be excluded from this offence. Last but not least, if the aforementioned pornographic material is held with the aim to exploit it for profit, the offender faces a sentence of 3 to 5 years in jail, a fine, or a combination of the two. And if the same offence is done again, the penalty is from 5 to 7 years in jail as well as a fine.

1. Under the Indian Penal Code, 1860

The Indian Penal Code does not specifically address child pornography, although section 293 of the code forbids the showing of offensive information to children. A young person in this context would be someone who is under the age of twenty. Therefore, sharing, disseminating, exhibiting, selling, or renting out any obscene material (as defined in section 292 IPC) to any young person would be illegal under Section 293 of the Code. On the first offence, the offender faces a maximum sentence of 3 years in jail and a fee of Rs. 2000; however, if convicted again, the maximum sentence increases to 7 years in prison and a fine of Rs. 5000.[2]

3. Under the Information Technology Act, 2000

The act of publishing, sending, making, collecting, browsing, downloading, advertising, promoting, trading, distributing, recording, etc. of any electronic media that depicts a sexually explicit action involving a minor is punishable under Section 67B of the IT Act. It also penalises the development of ties with any kid over the internet for sexually explicit acts and online child abuse. For a first conviction under Section 67B, the penalty is five years in jail and a fine of ten lakh rupees; for a second conviction, the penalty is seven years in prison and a payment of ten lakh rupees.[3]

[1]Protection of Children from Sexual Offences Act, 2012

[2]Indian Penal Code 1860

[3]Information of technology act 2000

CHAPTER ELEVEN

EFFECT OF COVID LOCKDOWN ON CHILD PORNOGRAPHY MARKET

The India Child Protection Fund (ICPF) report outed in April 2020 reported that there has been an escalation of 95% in consumption of child pornography material in India. This data has been cited from 'Pornhub', which is one of the biggest pornography websites all over the world.[1]

The majority of schools, universities, and offices were shuttered during the COVID-19 lockdown period. Due to the fact that all work and research was done online, a significant rise in the number of hours people spent online was observed. Without a question, if youngsters spend a lot of time online, in addition to using it for academic reasons, they will get familiar with all the facets of this cutting-edge digital technology. But when these innocent kids browse the internet, they are unaware of the sexual predators prowling the area looking for them. And the growing popularity of child porn is the sole reason these guys are targeting minors.

Paedophiles, child molesters, rapists, and other types of criminals all spent a lot more time online during the lockdown than they typically do. According to the ICPF research, there has been a sharp increase in searches for terms like "teen sex," "sexy child," etc. throughout this time. Such activities enhance the demand for materials featuring child sexual abuse, and in order to meet that need, the operators of child pornography networks will do whatever it takes to keep their clients informed and line their wallets with billions of dollars. This demand motivates the market's masters to engage in child sex abuse, child molestation, child trafficking, etc., leading to an increase in crime. Additionally, a recent report from

Childline India Helpline showed that they had received more than 90,000 calls asking how to keep kids safe from harm during the nationwide lockdown. This information makes it quite evident that there was a substantially increased danger of child abuse during this lockdown and that it will likely get worse.

[1](Child Protection India | India Child Protection Fund | Fund | Icpf |, n.d.)

CHAPTER TWELVE

CONCLUSION

The crime of child pornography is not simply one crime; rather, it is a string of crimes with severe penalties. The abuse starts when a youngster is sexually abused, and even if the child is aware of what is occurring, it still doesn't make things any better. Then, such abuse is documented and disseminated to certain abhorrent individuals who take great delight in seeing those youngsters suffer as a result of their exploitation, which motivates them to engage in such behaviour themselves. This is how people's desire to commit such horrible deeds develops, and many of them go on to succeed in doing so, leading to an increase in crime.

A kid is someone who is just beginning their life and still has many years to go, yet it becomes very difficult for that youngster to lead a normal life after being a victim of a crime as terrible as child pornography. Such an occurrence would permanently stigmatise the child's thinking. In a considerable proportion of incidents of child sexual abuse, it has also been discovered that the victims knew the perpetrators, who may be family members, acquaintances, teachers, etc. Such situations are considerably more upsetting since the youngster would have trusted the person in question and would not have predicted it to occur. What could be more depressing than the knowledge that the kids are not safe even in their own homes.

Without a question, the government has taken a number of measures to battle this scourge, including passing laws like the POCSO and IT Act that particularly address the problem of child pornography. Even though the government has outright prohibited the websites that occasionally host the offending content, the prevalence of child abuse has not decreased. Given the current situation, it is evident that the government will take an increasing number of steps to address this problem, but can anything be done to address this issue on a personal level.

Such crimes have a number of issues, one of which is that they go unreported since they are not discussed. It may thus be time for us to start talking about it and educating our kids about potential hazards so that when they do, they will approach us without fear. Every person has to have good sex education in order to avoid receiving insufficient instruction from outside sources and choosing a bad course of action.